Cinemavino,
Volume 1

CINEMAVINO, VOLUME 1

TODD WOFFORD

Contents

They may seem totally different, but wine and movies have one thing in common: Both can change us, in big ways and small. When we walk out of a theater, our lives have been altered. Maybe we chuckled through a stupid comedy, and then laughed at ourselves for laughing. Or a devastating drama shattered our souls and brought us to tears. Think about the greatest movies. You probably remember where you saw them, and who sat next to you. Hell, the worst movies can make just as strong of an impression. Either way, every film tells us a little more about the world, and our place within it.

Likewise, the story of wine spreads over thousands of years and hundreds of countries. Every bottle means something special to somebody somewhere. Every label has a story just waiting to be told. Yes, wine pairs with food, but you can actually match it with just about anything. A good book only gets better with a glass of wine. Ditto for a wedding toast. And a summer sunset. Or the smoky snaps of a fireplace during winter. A good glass of wine enhances, enriches, and deepens. Its story becomes part of yours.

For this book, we're gonna pair wine and movies. The vino could have some geographical tie, or maybe it's just *simpatico* to the plot in some way. In the case of *Monty Python and the Holy Grail*, the grape compliments one of the movie's funniest jokes. Either way, the wine will give you something extra to enjoy during the movie.

After a few glasses, you'll find that even the worst movies can become surprisingly watchable!

When it comes to wine reviews, I'll try to keep things brief and non-snooty. Wine has kind of a highfalutin reputation anyway, so the last thing anybody needs is some goofball blathering right over their heads. Also, most of these bottles fall somewhere between $10-30. If your local wine shop doesn't have a particular bottle, they should be able to steer you to something comparable.

I studied film in college, and managed a wine store for 14 years. This book combines two of my biggest passions into one space. I only hope you enjoy reading it as much as I enjoyed writing it.

As always, I'm indebted to my family and friends for their help and support. A special thanks goes to my wife Jo, who always finds a way to fill my sky with stars. We're a few weeks away from becoming parents, and I can't wait to see where that grand adventure takes us.

1.

Sideways (2004) -- Merlot

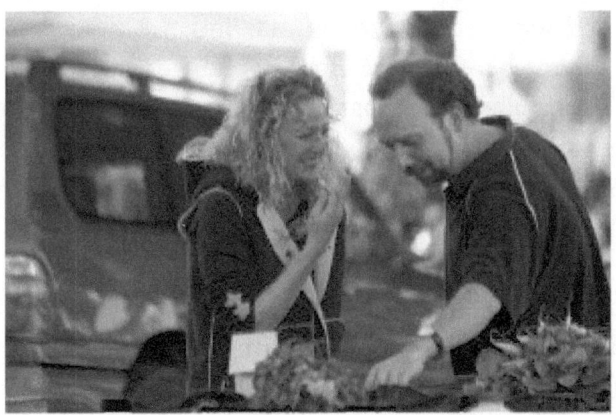

© 2004 20th Century Fox

For Miles Raymond, wine isn't just an outlet for all his eccentric passion, it's a hub around which his entire world spins. It nourishes all his best and worst traits at once: Wine invigorates and inspires him, while also supplying him with a limitless reservoir of hangovers and bad decisions. He savors a good Pinot Noir for all its patrician nuance, but then he overindulges to drown in his own sorrows. *Sideways* is often pegged as a movie about wine, but I would disagree. It's more about the quirky man who uses it as both his shield and sustenance. If Miles' life revolves around wine, then the movie—which mirrors its protagonist's frumpy humor and twitchy neuroses—revolves around him.

Based on the novel by Rex Pickett, *Sideways* depicts two middle-aged buddies at an important juncture in their lives. Miles (Paul Giamatti) is a high school teacher who sits in muffled misery while his students fumble through great literature. For years, Miles has been molding his own convoluted novel, and struggles to find a buyer for its esoteric contents. Jack (Thomas Haden Church), his lifelong friend, stands to be married the next weekend. Jack is a has-been actor, who's career peak resembles that of Joey Tribbiani in *Friends*: He had a nice run as a soap star, before settling into a career narrating oozy side effects in pharmaceutical commercials. The movie begins as these disparate souls unite for a bachelor week in wine country.

*Sideways*farms some big laughs out of the way each man responds to wine: For Miles, his initial sip is an anal-retentive ritual of slurping and swirling. Meanwhile, Jack gulps it down and smacks his gum. It's a perfect demonstration of two completely different personalities: Miles finds comfort in being fussy and obsessive, but Jack is just looking for another vacant good time. This foreshadows the deeper issues they bring with them for this trip. Miles is still wallowing in self-pity for his failed marriage, and Jack fears the eternal commitment of his own impending nuptials.

Both of these problems come to a head when Miles and Jack meet two women on their wine tour. Maya (Virginia Madsen) is a grounded, wine-loving divorcée who waitresses at Miles' favorite watering hole. Stephanie (Sandra Oh) pours at one of the wineries and immediately fires up a flirty banter with Jack. Everyone pairs off, but not without considerable tension: Miles fumes at Jack's philandering ways, while Jack is gobsmacked that Miles' self-destructive grumpiness might prevent him from an opportunity to move on and be happy.

All the ingredients are present for a dark character study, but *Sideways* manages to keep it light. As with his other films, director Alexander Payne mines humor from quiet moments and big, broad set pieces. One example lies in how Miles can be finicky and pretentious with wine, but that completely disappears during his many emotional meltdowns. During one scene, Miles ravenously downs the spit bucket, with the fury of the Cookie Monster tearing into a sleeve of Thin Mints. It's a great example of how Payne takes drama and quickly pivots it toward humor.

As for the performances, Giamatti and Church fire off each other so easily, you'd think this was their 10th movie together. Honestly, all the main actors deliver Oscar-worthy performances. The famous scene where Miles and Maya share why they love wine is a master class in great acting: Madsen's Maya speaks with casual joy, as if she relishes the chance to finally open up about herself. In response, Giamatti gives Miles a face of fascination and fear. Their attraction could be real, but he wants to run for the hills anyway.

Sideways has plenty of great wines, but they mainly add shading and depth to the story. The proof lies in that you don't have to know a damn thing about wine to think this is a great movie. Wine just gives these characters a reason to speak poetically about what they love and hide their vulnerabilities in plain sight. *Sideways* is one of the sharpest, funniest, and quietly inspirational movies about human nature ever made.

127 min. R.

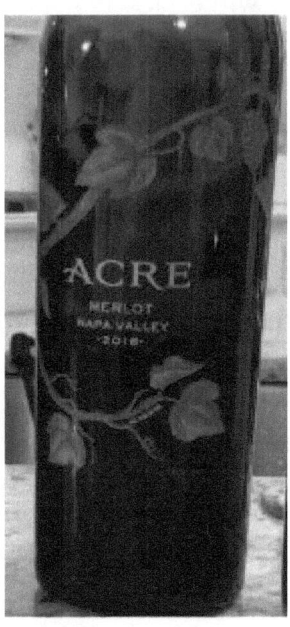

MERLOT

"If anybody orders Merlot, I'm leaving. I'm not drinking any *f*cking Merlot!!!!*" — Miles Raymond, *Sideways*

Has any single line of dialogue ever killed anything the way Paul Giamatti's Miles plunges a serrated dagger into the purple heart of Merlot? Frightened wine buyers quietly sent their Merlot stash gurgling down the garbage disposal, and they've hardly stopped in the years since.

The Merlot section in your favorite wine store probably shrank quite a bit. Winemakers worldwide felt the pain.

The crazy thing about this poisonous jab? It's total BS. And if Miles could do a couple of deep knee bends, he would agree with me. Devotees of the book upon which *Sideways* is based will tell you that Miles doesn't hate Merlot because it sucks. He hates it because his ex-wife loved to drink it. Miles refuses to enjoy his prized '61 Cheval Blanc because it's a Merlot blend they were supposed to share.

It's time for this prejudice against Merlots to die. If this grape makes you think of craggy old ladies drinking liquefied cardboard and spouting gibberish at daytime talk shows, well...you're wrong. Merlot is an Old World, old money wine. It's one of the major components in red Bordeaux. There are plenty of kickass Merlots out there, and if you're ignoring them because of one cinematic curmudgeon's moment of blind rage, you're missing out.

The 2016 **Acre Merlot** is an elegant, approachable example of everything great about the varietal: It's full-bodied yet satin-smooth. The tannins are there, but they never overwhelm the palate. Instead, you might catch some pronounced earthiness and dried, dark fruit flavor. The finish is so smooth it might as well come with a thread count. It could enhance a hearty meal–lamb would be a great choice–or make a fun standalone bottle for your guests.

A wine this good could transform Merlot into your go-to choice.

2.

Network (1976) --
Malbec

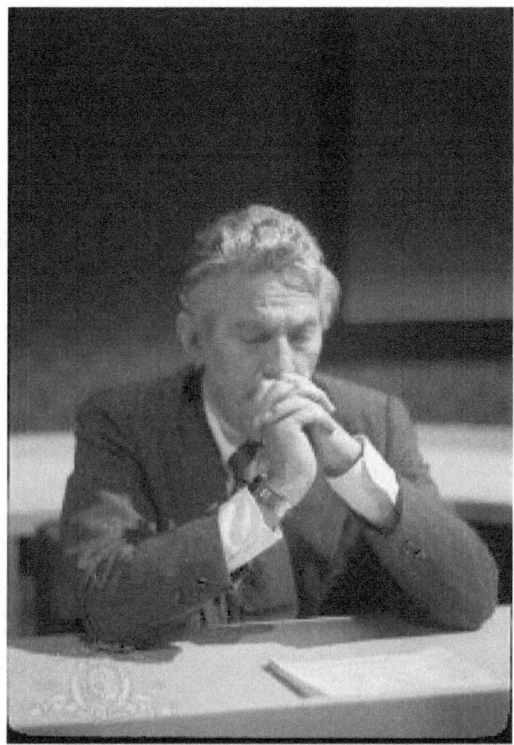

© Metro-Goldwyn-Mayer Studios Inc

By 1976, television had already gained momentum as a cultural hurricane, churning and demolishing everything in its path. No film predicted the tack that storm would take better than *Network*. Audiences who once laughed with nervous energy at the lunacy of blood-soaked infotainment now cringe that its satirical apocalypse has been fully realized. Frothing pundits now command the airwaves, spouting pedantic demagoguery that makes Howard Beale sound Shakespearean by comparison. Grotesque cycles of 24-hour news batter us with relentless fury, until we can only stand in the sloshing wreckage and wait for the next onslaught. Every rewatching of *Network* makes one thing certain: We had plenty of advance warning.

The story centers on Howard Beale (Peter Finch), a shambling sheepdog of a man who anchors a fourth-place network news show. Howard is fired in the film's opening scenes, an act that takes away everything he has, but also gives him nothing to lose. Boozy and broken, Howard hijacks the following broadcast to announce his plans to commit on-air suicide. He predicts a massive audience, and he's absolutely right: Millions of people, frightened and curious, tune in for Howard's profanity-laden diatribe. The network, sensing a hit, keeps him on the air and encourages him to "articulate the popular rage."

A carnival atmosphere springs up around Howard, and we see several characters with disparate enthusiasm for living within its cacophony: Max (William Holden) is the news director, and Howard's best friend. Frank (Robert Duvall) serves as a corporate hatchet man and the serpentine influence who guides Howard along the path of certain destruction. Diana (Faye Dunaway), the icy new programming director, approaches her mandate to put the network in the black with Machiavellian cruelty.

Of these characters, Max shows the deepest emotional and ethical conflict: He's torn between a growing concern for Howard's obvious breakdown and an almost primal fascination with Diana's redoubtable ruthlessness. As the movie's moral center, Max attempts to simultaneously save Howard and sate his rusty sense of lust, and he fails on both fronts.

Network is a shimmering showcase of stars, but none shine brighter than screenwriter Paddy Chayefsky. His brilliant, boiling dialogue rolls through the movie like lava, searing each scene with its dramatic intensity. It's refreshing to see a movie unafraid to give us characters who can speak with such passion and intelligence. Director Sidney Lumet, already known for his restraint, wisely lets Chayefsky's script take first chair.

If Chayefsky's dialogue is like a well-seasoned steak from Morton's, then it's no surprise that this cast of Oscar-winners chow down on it. Two big monologues have earned their place in cinema lore: Howard's wild onscreen jeremiad in which he pleads with viewers to go outside and vent their frustrations to the sky: "I'm mad as hell, and I'm not going to take this anymore!" Finch's face quivers maniacally and he raises his hands to the air, like a batshit street preacher. The other moment occurs when Ned Beatty shows up as a tycoon who attempts to set Howard straight about how his rants are affecting the flow of currency: "The world is a business, Mr. Beale. It has been since man crawled out of the slime." It's an expansive tirade that has a strange, musical poetry to it. Beatty has had some big scenes in some big movies, but this might be his best work ever. In fact, every performance here is a master class in acting.

Famed director Howard Hawks once observed that a good movie should have three good scenes and no bad scenes. *Network* has at least ten really good scenes and zero bad scenes. There's not one false moment, nor one syllable of dialogue that feels out of place. Every bit of satire lands exactly where it's supposed to, and the movie maintains its dour worldview all the way to the memorable closing shot. I have a short list of absolutely perfect movies, and this is one of them. *Network* is a story both of and beyond its time. It looked ahead and saw that we would maintain our love affair with television, right up to the moment it leveled us to the ground.

121 min. R.

MALBEC

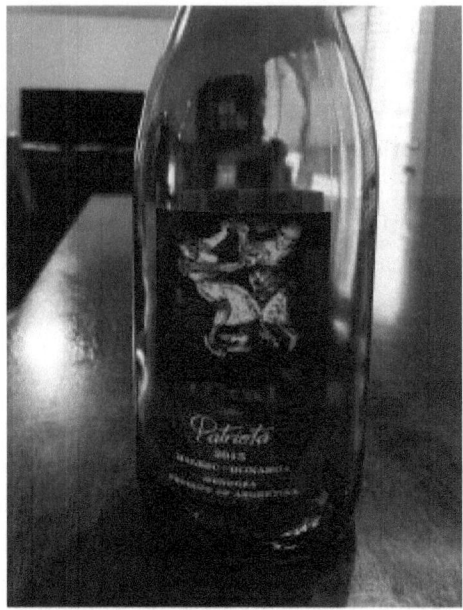

Network is a strange, brilliant comedy: Bleak in outlook, bone-dry in delivery, so many scenes in this movie are somehow funny and ominous at the same time. Movie history is replete with black comedies, but this one rules them all.

It just makes sense to pair the sarcastic savagery of *Network* with a wine that can match its dark tone and texture. A Malbec sounds like the perfect fit. Known as one of the five varietals that make up red Bordeaux, Malbecs are the primary component of reds from the Cahors region of France. That being said, the popular association with Malbec lies with Argentina. So, to fit the bill for *Network*, we'll venture to South America.

The **Patriota Malbec** from Tikal is an excellent bottle of wine. Deep purple in color, heavy in body, this Argentine red is balances broad, earthy notes with robust flavors of currant and ground pepper. Translation: It's dry yet fruity, big but approachable. Like many Malbecs, this will pair well with big meals, such as steak or lamb. From a cinematic standpoint, the Patriota Malbec makes a perfect match with the rich, brawny humor of *Network*.

3.

The Good, the Bad and the Ugly (1966) -- Albariño

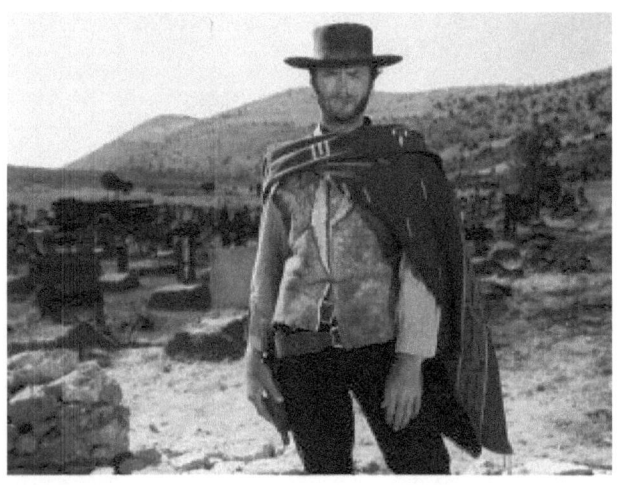

There's a moment early on in *The Good, the Bad and the Ugly* when Clint Eastwood's panchoed badass strolls into frame, lights a thin cigar, and scowls for the camera. In that instant of savage cool, the Monument Valley Western was forever demolished. John Wayne's false-modest bravado and Jimmy Stewart's hem-haw heroics couldn't have felt more antiquated. Sergio Leone's masterpiece makes it official: The frontier is now the dominion of the anti-hero.

This might seem like a strange comparison, but I can't escape it: What the Beatles did for rock music, Leone did for the Western. Both of those genres were settled and stale, to the point they were almost parodies of themselves. Like the Moptops, Leone took something he loved and shook it like a snow globe. The result was something new, infused with an essential dose of European post-modernism and some irresistible cockiness.

The Good, the Bad and the Ugly is the ultimate embodiment of Sergio Leone's auteurism: At three hours, its simplicity is sweeping in scope. Long stretches amble in stylish silence, as characters swagger and stare through puffs of cigar smoke Much of this wordlessness gets filled with Ennio Morricone's phenomenal soundtrack, which sets a series of crow-caws and menacing whistles to the pounding of a jungle war-drum.

Our story focuses on three disparate men plunk in a desperate quest: The American Civil War rages, and a Confederate cashbox has vanished somewhere in the New Mexican badlands. Angel Eyes (Lee Van Cleef) is an icy thief who will kill anybody anywhere to find the money. Eli Wallach's Tuco is a loud-mouthed *bandito* who always seems to be in the wrong place at the right time, or vice versa. The Man with No Name (Clint Eastwood) has the least twitchy trigger, and in this cast of rapscallions, that qualifies him as the hero.

That might not sound like enough to prop up 178 minutes of movie, but Leone's infectiously eccentric touch makes the time fly. The script may be light on dialogue, but the world-class trio of leads put the right spin on every syllable. If the earlier *Dollars* movies proved that Eastwood could carry a movie, *Good* shows that he has enough star power to put the entire Western genre onto his shoulders. His performance isn't just good or great, but the stuff of legends: Rarely has a superstar shot so high with such lean material.

Ol' Clint ain't alone, neither. Few character actors convey menace with the alarming twinkle of Lee Van Cleef, and his Angel Eyes is a mastered mix of cheerful and monstrous. Meanwhile, Wallach runs off with every scene he's in, like a running back in the open field. Few performances have settled into Leone's groove of self-assured silliness with the efficiency of Wallach's ornery bastard. Leone and Eastwood get a lot of the glory, but this movie truly feels like a team effort.

The Good, the Bad and the Ugly isn't just a Spaghetti Western. It's *the* Spaghetti Western. Filmed on gorgeous Spanish and Italian locales, Leone rewrites in the rules, and he does it in style. The overrated *Man Who Shot Liberty Valance* proved that John Ford's hokum had finally outlived its relevance, and it was past time for something different. *The Good, the Bad and the Ugly* reminds us that if you want to start over, sometimes all it takes is a fistful of dynamite.

178 min. Not Rated.

ALBARIÑO

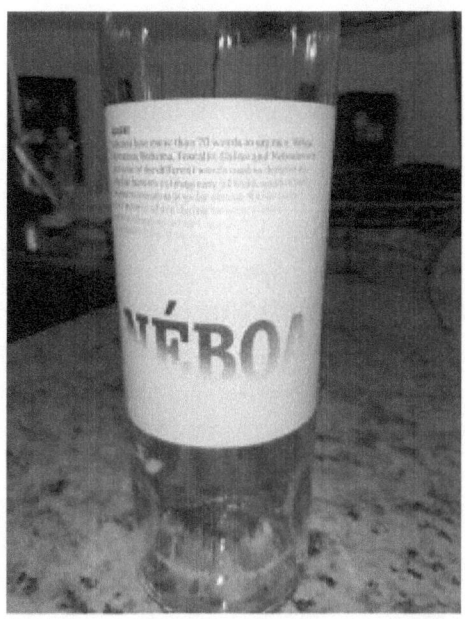

It may sound like a paradox, but *The Good, the Bad and the Ugly* is truly an international Western: Sergio Leone's *tour de force* was filmed in Italy and Spain, with an Italian crew and American leads. *And* it's set in New Mexico during the American Civil War. This makes it a cinematic melting pot, where many different viewpoints come together to make something even better.

Many of Leone's brick-brown vistas can be found in the Spanish countryside. Spain has a rich, distinct heritage of wine, and that makes it easy to find something to pair with this classic movie.

The Albariño grape can be found across the Iberian Peninsula. In Spain, Albariños are commonly found in the Rías Baixas region, located in the Northwestern part of the country. Though it can now be grown in other countries (including the United States), this grape is still closely associated with both Spain and Portugal.

Nêboa's **Albariño** is a classic expression of the varietal: It's fresh and floral, with pronounced acidity right from the first sip. Like many Spanish (and French) whites, this one has a limestone flavor that helps balance out its peachy textures. The acid levels off on the finish, making this an easy-drinking white. Looking to pair with a meal? Try some sushi or shrimp.

Nêboa not only fits the geography of *The Good, the Bad and the Ugly*, it also pairs with its climate. The main characters sweat and stumble across sun-baked sand. It can make you overheat just watching them. A chilled, refreshing white wine is just what you need.

4.

Four Weddings and a Funeral (1993) -- Bubbly and Scotch

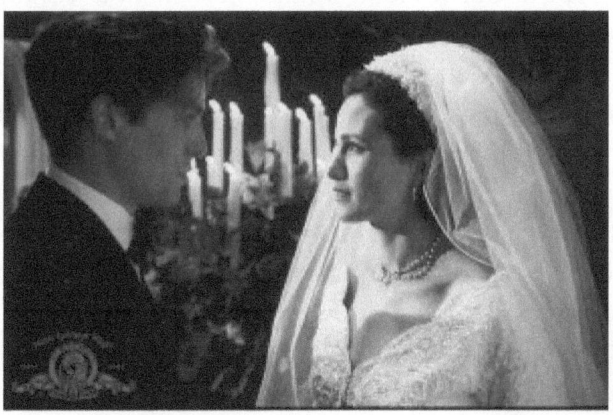

© 1994 Metro-Goldwyn-Mayer Studios Inc.

So much of dating feels like trying on a new wardrobe: You have to see the awkwardness of someone who doesn't fit correctly to truly appreciate the magic of someone who does. The characters in *Four Weddings and a Funeral* spend their time in fidgety frustration, waiting for the person who will add a fairy tale ending to their lives. They attend a slew of weddings with an uneasy blend of anticipation and dread. A soulmate could be out there, hanging on the same rack with one-night-stands and toxic relationships.

As the title suggests, the entire plot follows this rowdy band of lovable ragamuffins as they move from one big social event to the next. Charles (Hugh Grant) serves as the group's de facto leader, probably because he has movie star looks and a fair amount of dweebish charisma. Each member of his clique can be distinguished as such: Fiona (Kristin Scott Thomas) is the lovely, lonely girl who carries a lifelong torch for Charles. Tom (James Fleet) plays the resident fool. Gareth (Simon Callow) and Matthew (John Hannah) are the ebullient gay couple. Scarlett (Charlotte Coleman) gives the squad a wild card. With each new wedding, our heroes load up like clowns in a Volkswagen and go hunting for love, wherever it may be.

At the first wedding, Charles is gobsmacked when he meets Carrie (Andie MacDowell), a beautiful, charming American woman. The resulting sparks supply the movie with its throughline: Could this instant reaction lead to something lasting? If what they have is true love, can it truly overcome all? Charles and Carrie fall in and out of touch and date other people, but those electric feelings never seem to go away.

The weddings mix wry observations about finding and maintaining relationships with some proper British silliness: A loony vicar (Rowan Atkinson) fumbles his way through the vows at a ceremony, while Charles forgets the rings at another. He also gets stranded at a reception table populated with seething ex-girlfriends, and later has to (in what feels like a *Fawlty Towers* outtake) hide in a hotel room closet just as the newlyweds stumble in for a giddy, screaming roll in the hay. Much of *Four Weddings* is filled with such gentle, easy humor.

If the farcical weddings fill the movie with fluff, then the funeral supplies an emotional center. A key character dies, forcing everyone in the group to take a sober assessment of what they really want. For Charles, this means wavering between a safe relationship with an annoying ex–who is, appropriately, named Hen–and the brilliant rapport he has with Carrie. This conflict continues until the movie's Wow Finish. People have labeled this last scene as corny and over-the-top, but I think anything less would've let the movie down.

At the same time, I have to agree this movie has a few flaws, and they grow more apparent with every viewing. Hugh Grant hems and haws to a maddening degree. Some of his dialogue is delivered with the twitchy timidity of a sweaty man diffusing a nuclear bomb. Just cut the god damn blue wire and move on. MacDowell also has some bizarre line readings, as if her speaking voice has been robbed of its usual pitch and rhythm.

And yet, I still wanted this couple to get together forever. Maybe it's the clever, breezy script from Richard Curtis, or the solid comic timing of most of the cast. Whatever the case, this movie works and has held up remarkably well. I saw this movie as a child, and I enjoyed it in a broad sort of way. It was goofy and cute. But I didn't really appreciate it until my 20s and 30s, when I got to experience being a groomsman, an usher, and a best man. As I watched my friends marry off, I could suddenly relate to the joy and jealousy, the excitement and anxiety that Charles feels with each passing wedding. That time of life was an unparalleled adventure, but this movie also reminds me why I'm glad it's over.

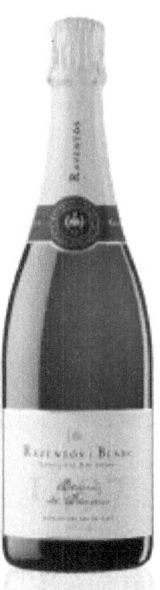

BUBBLY

When people think of bubbly, two wild extremes come to mind. On one hand, you might picture a tweedy snob with a twiddly mustache, swirling and slurping some authentic French Champagne. Of course, there's also the cheap swill, which mainly exists to round out brunch mimosas and fuel bad decisions at weddings and New Year's Eve parties. Fortunately, between that divide lies a happy middle ground: Many sparkling wines are out there that don't require taking out a second mortgage, *and* won't give you a soul-crushing hangover.

My wife Joanna and I went to Spain for our honeymoon, and we had the pleasure of touring this outstanding winery. Located near the town of Sant Sadurni d'Anoia,

Raventós captures many of the great things about Spain in one place: The people are friendly, the scenery is beautiful, and the wine is some of the best in the world. For this review, we'll be taking a look at their Blanc de Blanc.

The Blanc de Blanc from Raventós is a prime example of this win-win scenario. It has the same limestone notes you'll find in Southern France, but also textures of anis, lemon, and a hint of melon flavor. That finish is so smooth and crisp, it practically begs for another sip. A fashion metaphor perfectly describes a bottle like this: Raventós is that pair of jeans you can dress up or down. It's complex and attractive enough for a wedding toast or an anniversary dinner, but also approachable and affordable for a patio night with you and your crew.

Ps. If you have a chance to see Raventós in person, I'd highly recommend it. It's a postcard-perfect locale with a proud history dating to 1497. They do tastings and tours by appointment, so you'll want to hit them up before you go.

Facebook and Instagram: @raventosiblanc

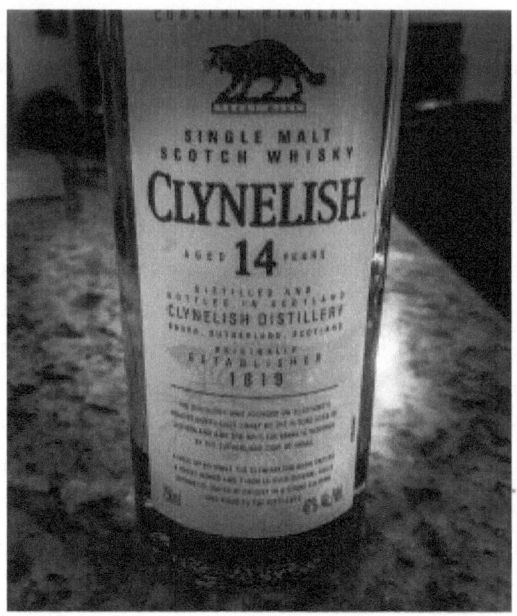

SCOTCH

As the title suggests, a somber ceremony sits plunk in the middle of *Four Weddings and a Funeral*. It drenches the daffy revelers in the movie with a cold blast of water. So, now that I've given you a bubbly to toast your favorite characters with, here's a little whiskey to drown your sorrows alongside them.

The 14-year-old single malt from **Clynelish** from the Central Highlands, and it has a few characteristics to distinguish it from its geographical brethren: Peaty, salty are quickly apparent to the nose and mouth, before giving way to notes of toasted almonds, hints of earthiness, and a floral finish. This is a well-rounded Scotch, with something in its flavor profile for fans of just about every region. A spritz of water mellows it out considerably. Pair this with a roaring fireplace, a post-dinner porch session, or whenever you to need to raise a glass for a departed character in a beloved movie.

Someday, when I inevitably shuffle off this mortal coil, I don't want to be remembered with some mopey affair. Quite the opposite, in fact: My final wish would be for my loved ones to counter the sobering impact of my demise with a few good stories and a stiff drink to wash them down. Every mourner at every memorial where booze is served can probably think of a specific drink with some connection to the deceased. However, in the absence of that info, a good bottle of Scotch always makes a fine choice.

5.

Children of Men (2006) -- Red Bordeaux

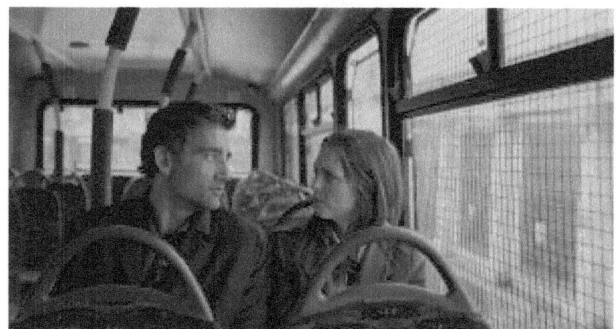

Copyright: Universal Studios

Ancient wisdom tells us that all things end, but solace can be found in the continuation of the whole. Put another way: Life goes on. But what if it doesn't? *Children of Men* shows us a near-future where global infertility has stripped the world of hope and purpose. On the surface, this is a blistering action thriller with groundbreaking direction and cinematography. Look below all that and you'll find where *Children of Men*'s real brilliance lies: This is a savvy and sobering study of human nature, and the great and terrible things we might do in the face of extinction.

Based on a novel by P.D. James, the movie is set in 2027. No babies have born in twenty years, causing civilization to rend itself to shreds. Tattered refugees wander the planet; lawlessness and abject poverty have swept over every continent. The United Kingdom stands as the last remnant of what was, and even it is barely recognizable. A fascist regime rules with clinical brutality.

Our story centers on Theo (Clive Owen), a once-passionate activist who is now a miserable, hard-drinking functionary. His downward spiral gets interrupted by the arrival of Julian (Julianne Moore). She's his ex-wife, and the charismatic leader of an underground movement. Julian pleads with Theo to use his connections to help Kee (Claire-Hope Ashitey), a young refugee in desperate need of sanctuary. He refuses, but circumstances draw him into the crisis. Theo is staggered to learn that Kee has to be smuggled to safety because she's *pregnant*. Undoubtedly, many people would like to exploit Kee and her baby for their own gain, so Theo joins the attempt to get Kee to people who can help her.

Most the movie boils with tension, as it hurtles from one bravura action beat to the next. Director Alfonso Cuarón stages these scenes masterfully, such as a car chase that takes place in a seemingly unbroken take. As with his incredible *Roma*, Cuarón lets the camera run (CGI edits add to the illusion) as if it's meant to bear witness to these unbelievable events. The final gun battle evokes *Saving Private Ryan* with its blood-soaked savagery.

The script (by a team of writers) excels because it takes a look at how tragic events bring out the uglier sides of humanity. People cast blame in all directions; xenophobia spreads like a disease. The government imposes fertility tests on its citizens, and herds immigrants into concentration camps. More than anything, *Children of Men* takes a hard look at how we act in our darkest moments, and how much those actions define us.

It's rare to see a movie so genuinely exciting and fearlessly intelligent at once. This is also one of the few movies that will show you new things upon every viewing. *Children of Men* will leave you exhausted, inspired, and contemplative–quite the triple crown for any piece of entertainment. This is one of the best films of the last twenty years.

109 min. R.

BORDEAUX

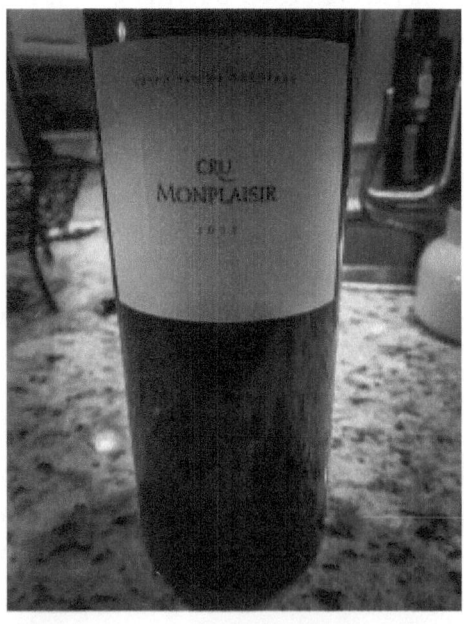

Reds from Bordeaux are complex, heavy wines, so it makes sense to pair one with an intense, deeply philosophical movie. *Children of Men* blends thought-provoking drama with pounding action scenes, so only the hardiest of wines can stand up to it.

First a little background: Located in Southwestern France, Bordeaux is one of the oldest wine-growing regions in the world. (Romans brought grapes here sometime in the First Century.) And, like everywhere else in France, wine names are geography-specific. *Only* wines from this area can be called Bordeaux. Similarly, only specific grapes are allowed in a bottle. Red wines from Bordeaux are comprised of five classic varietals: Cabernet, Merlot, Cabernet Franc, Petit Verdot, and Malbec. (Carmenere can be found in small amounts, but this is pretty rare.) Most of these are some combo of Cab, Merlot, and Cabernet Franc.

The 2015 **Cru Monplaisir** is an approachable, affordable ($20ish) bottle from one of the most intimidating regions in the world. It's mostly Merlot, with a little Cab Franc and Cab to add a little oomph. Dark, dry currant flavor is immediately apparent, as is a broadly earthy undertone. This is complemented by a finish that's both velvety and floral, making this wine seem big and easy-drinking, all at once.

If wine regions were cars, then Bordeaux would be a Rolls Royce. Bottles from that region have earned a reputation for being elegant, sturdy, and timeless. And expensive. Indeed, many of the fanciest and most famous red wines in all the world hail from this region in France. That being said, you can also find many offerings that won't immolate your bank statement.

(There are also many delicious whites from Bordeaux.

These are comprised of some blend of Sauvignon Blanc, Sémillon, and Muscadelle. But that's a whole other kettle of fish.)

A footnote: The British will often refer to a Bordeaux as a Claret. American wines that are grown in the style of this region are sometimes called Meritage wines. (It rhymes with "heritage.")

6.

The Third Man (1948) -- Various Austrian Wines

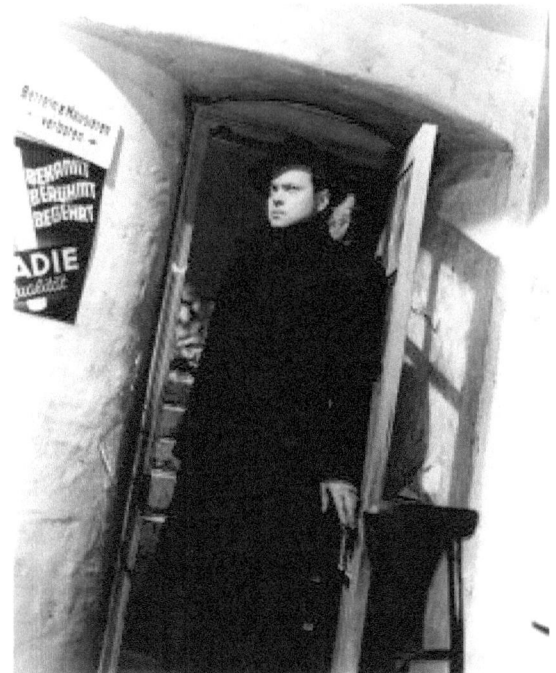

© Courtesy: Rialto Pictures/Studiocanal

In the immediate aftermath of World War II, Vienna stood as a nexus where soot-stained cynicism met and mingled with nefarious opportunity. Like most of Europe, Austria struggled to rebuild after the destruction of the Third Reich. Industry was hobbled; food and medicine became scarce. *The Third Man*, one of the most beautiful and tightly constructed mysteries ever made, deploys this beleaguered atmosphere as a supporting character unto itself. Characters lurk in dark corners and creep through sewers and alleyways, their shadows dancing like ghosts on the cobblestones. This is a film of and beyond its time, bridging the refinements of classics such as *Casablanca* and *Citizen Kane* with the progressively darker storylines that would dominate American *film noir*, the French New

Wave and eventually help demolish Hollywood's archaic Production Code.

The story begins as Holly Martins (Joseph Cotton), a writer of Zane Grey-style paperbacks, arrives in Vienna. His old buddy, Harry Lime, has sent for him with the promise of finding work. Martins has no sooner set foot in the city only to find that Lime has been killed under mysterious circumstances. Determined, Martins begins to untangle the unsavory details of his friend's life and death, including his involvement in the Viennese black market and his relationship with Anna, an emotionally fragile Czech actress (Alida Valli). One of the joys of the film is watching Cotton's character struggle through a parade of contradicting witnesses, menacing cops, and urbane thugs who toy with him and plot his destruction. And like any great mystery, the script unveils many clever (and very, *very* imitated) plot twists.

Though Orson Welles did not direct this film (he only plays a supporting character), the stylistic innovations of his early work radiate throughout. The camera tilts into Dutch angles, casting unnaturally long shadows and underlining the moral ambiguity of almost every character. This film ranks alongside *Citizen Kane* (and *Touch of Evil later*) as one of the finest examples of black and white cinematography. Several shots stand as self-contained masterpieces, such as Welles' character introduction, his eventual attempt to escape a sewer grate (with his fingers desperately wriggling into the air above), and the final shot of a lonely woman bisecting a barren dirt road. These pockets of cinematic perfection would be hailed and discussed by critics if they were in a *contemporary* movie, let alone 70 years ago.

The Third Man is one of those rare works that can be

enjoyed on multiple levels, and via many viewings. It occupies a distinguished patch on the quilt of film history: Welles' (self-written) Ferris wheel monologue, Anton Karas' rollicking (and *maddeningly* catchy) zither theme, and the final chase scene—they have to be seen by any serious movie buff. Beyond that, you can sense the influence it would have on a million directors who came after, from Truffaut and Goddard to Spielberg and Scorsese.

93 min. Not Rated.

AUSTRIAN WINES

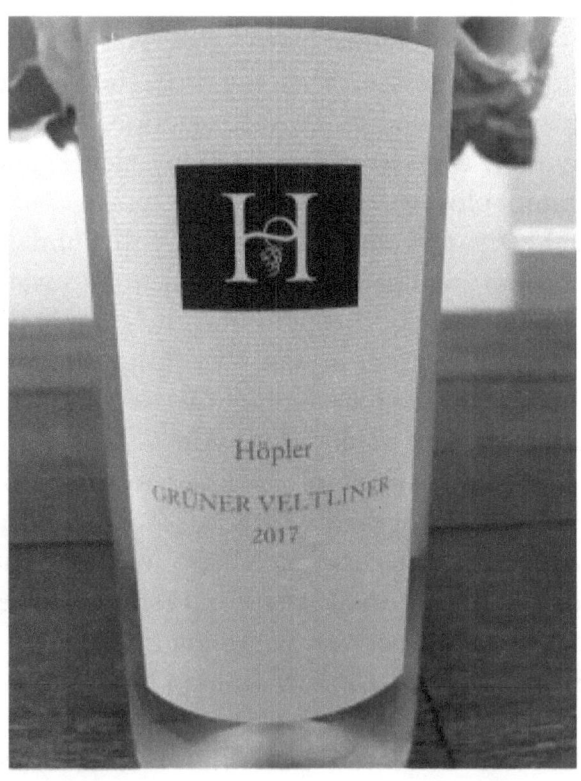

Höpler Grüner Veltiner – 2017

Grüner Veltiner is the most prevalent white wine in Austria, and this offering from Höpler will show you why. It's citrusy up front, and rounded off with pear and spicy notes as it goes down. The finish has a creamy texture that smoothes out any acidity. This is a velvety, easy-drinking bottle that shows why Grüners are catching on with white wine drinkers!

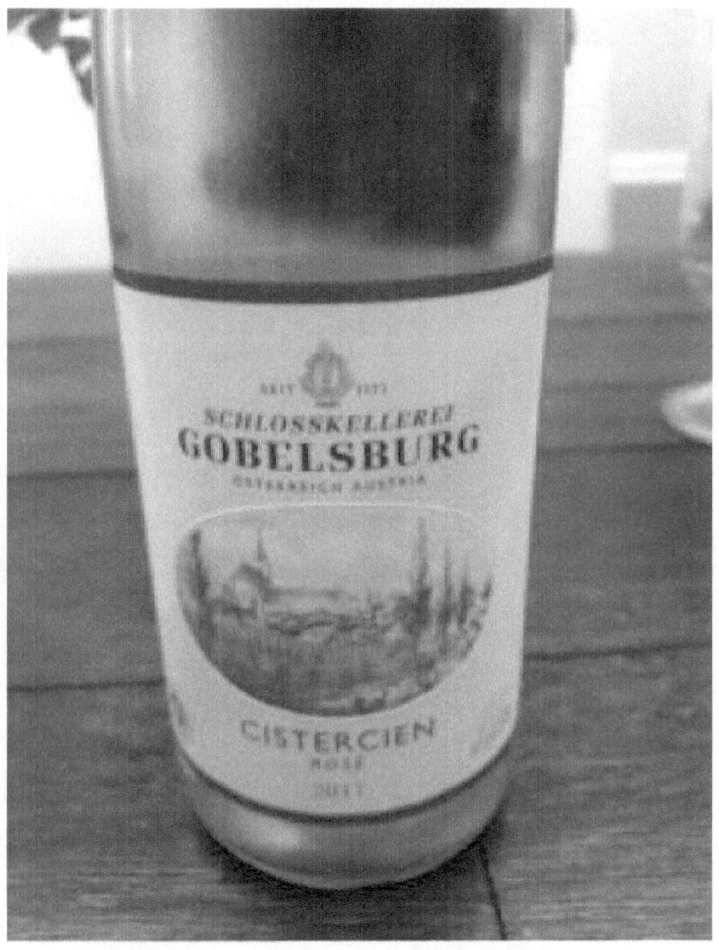

Schloss Gobelsburg Cistercien Rose – 2017

Like twist-off tops, rosé is still trying to shake off the bad rep bestowed on it by White Zin. This wine has about as much in common with White Zinfandel as *Lawrence of Arabia* has with *Spice World*. It's lean–"austere" is the snooty word we'll use–and fruity. (Wine can be fruity but not sweet, by the way.) Cherries and uh...honeydew! That's what it is. The finish is clean and floral. This is one of the most refreshing rosés out there, and it's pretty affordable to boot.

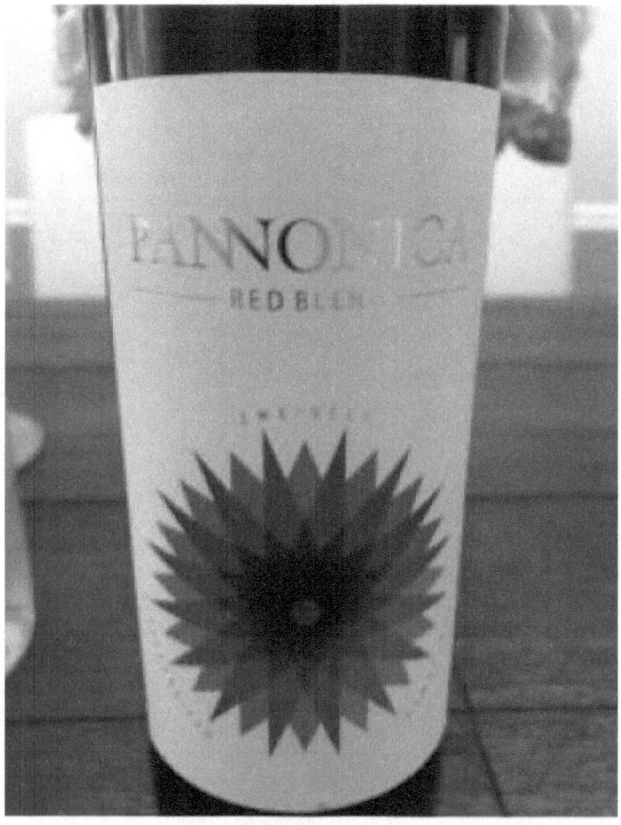

Pannonica Red Blend – 2017
    This dude melds three of the most common reds found

in Austria into one frighteningly cheap and flavorful bottle. A blend of Zweigelt, Blaufränkisch, and Pinot Noir, the Pannonica is loaded with notes of dark berries and earthy notes. It lightens up and smoothes out on the end, like it's challenging you to drink more. (And I will, damn you.) They don't make nearly as many Austrian reds as whites, and many are bigger and bolder than this one, but Pannonica's Red is an above-average everyday wine.

7.

Bull Durham (1988) -- Rosé and Beer

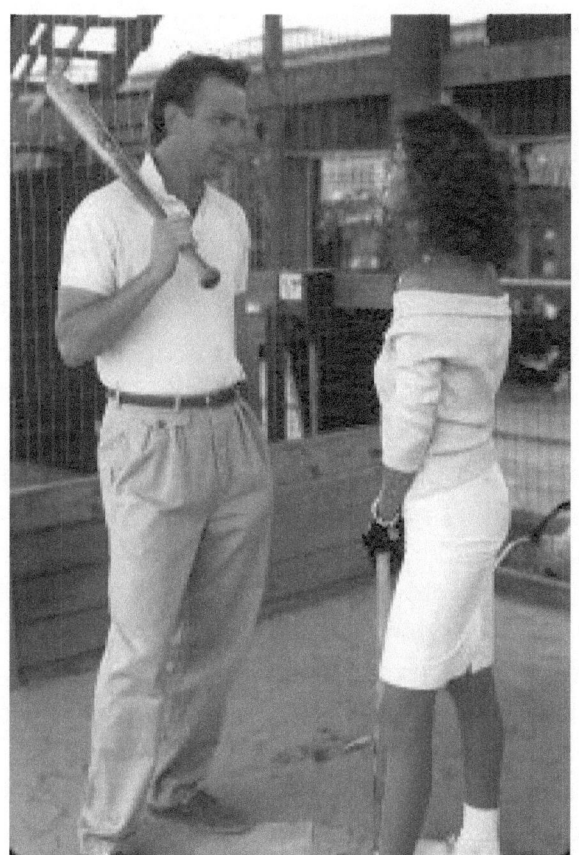

© 1988 Metro-Goldwyn-Mayer Studios Inc.

"This is a simple game. You throw the ball. You catch the ball. You hit the ball!" — Skip Riggins, Manager of the Durham Bulls.

The irony of the above statement is that *Bull Durham* centers on two characters who embody the exact opposite of its sentiment. For Crash Davis (Kevin Costner) and Annie Savoy (Susan Sarandon), baseball isn't just a sport of hits and pitches. It's a mystical, sweeping religion, replete with its own mythologies and superstitions. These two approach their faith from opposite angles: Crash is a weary cynic whom the game didn't bother to bless with both hands. For Annie, baseball represents an ever-flowing fountain of wisdom and salvation.

Durham focuses on one sweltering season for the Durham Bulls, a struggling minor league team. Things get spicy with the arrival of Ebby "Nuke" LaLoosh (Tim Robbins), a major league prospect with a million dollar arm and feathers in his head. A lovable, mercurial doofus, Nuke's fastball is just as likely to decapitate the mascot as find home plate. Crash is given a daunting assignment: Sand off Nuke's rough edges and give him the survival skills to endure the nomadic life of a professional athlete. Annie, who mentors one ballplayer every season, takes on a similar assignment. Her guidance, however, has elements of Eastern religion and intense sexuality.

Much of what follows will deal with the push and pull between these three characters: Nuke is caught between Annie's spiritual potpourri and Crash's real-world wisdom. Annie finds herself attracted to Nuke's guileless affability and Crash's worn-in worldliness. Crash fears that the heat between he and Annie is something real, while slowly developing a brotherly affection for Nuke's deceptively intelligent personality. As Nuke's star ascends, Crash's streaks to the ground, and all Annie can do is watch with worried fascination.

Bull Durham is widely acclaimed as one of the greatest of all sports movies, and this reputation is well-earned. Writer-director Ron Shelton (who played a bit of professional baseball himself) crafts sharp dialogue, and the lead actors savor every syllable of it. Costner's Crash walks and talks with a casual swagger, alternately tearing down Nuke before building him right back up again. Nuke's bravado is vacant and fragile, and Robbins is hilarious as a man who screws up song lyrics and babbles to himself on the pitcher's mound. ("Why's he keep callin' me 'Meat'? I'm the guy drivin' a Porsche.") As a mercenary girlfriend and amateur guru, Sarandon gives Annie a blend of wild-eyed brilliance, vulnerable pride, and unbound passion. Few other sports movies have performances like this and a script this good.

Perhaps the greatest thing about this movie is the ending. Audiences generally demand to feel good when they walk out of a sports film. Think of *Hoosiers*, or *Rudy*. People getting carried off the field. The soundtrack swelling as the screen fades to black. *Bull Durham* eschews all that for the poetry of realism: All things must end, and sometimes those endings come with a quiet melancholy. *Bull Durham* is the best sports movie because it shows how the game isn't just a matter of throwing, catching, and hitting. In its finest moments, baseball gives us a glimpse into who we really are.

108 min. R.

ROSÉ

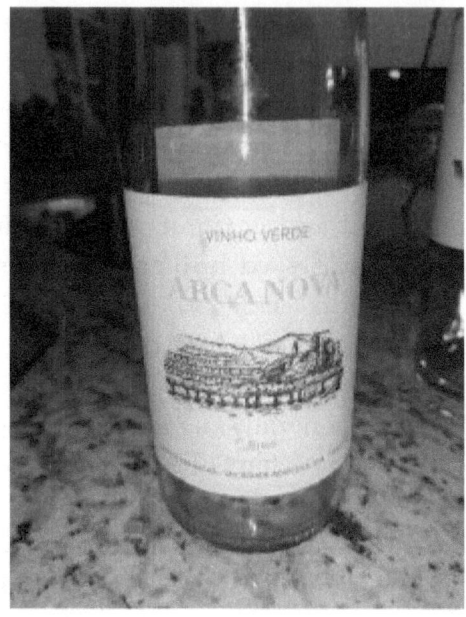

When a lot of people think of Rosé, they still picture a wine for old ladies. White Zin. Blush. Something the Golden Girls might enjoy with a slice of cheesecake out on the lanai. That reputation is as outdated as the Macarena. After all, the Rosé section in your local wine store has probably expanded in recent years. And most of those wines aren't syrupy bottles meant for Mahjong and *Matlock* reruns. Rosés are versatile, and criminally underrated. If you're not into them, now's a good time to start.

Although it gets bookended by the chill of spring and fall, baseball is largely a sweltering summer sport. It may've been filmed in cooler weather, but *Bull Durham* feels like a steamy movie. Characters climb in and out of bed together, share humid bus rides, and melt in the dugout and on the mound. A hot movie calls for a hot wine, so let's take a look at this Portuguese Rosé.

Arca Nova's Vinho Verde Rosé seems made for the summertime. It has some sweetness, but it's still not hummingbird feed. Pluck several fruit slices from a serving tray during a July block party, and that's what's you get here. Cantaloupe, strawberry, honeydew, and maybe even a hint of green apple can be found all the way through the finish. As for food pairings, pretty much anything you would chow down on at that block party: Fried chicken, burgers, shrimp, or even a plate of onion rings. Think you can't have a good bottle of wine during a barbecue or a ball game? It's time to think again.

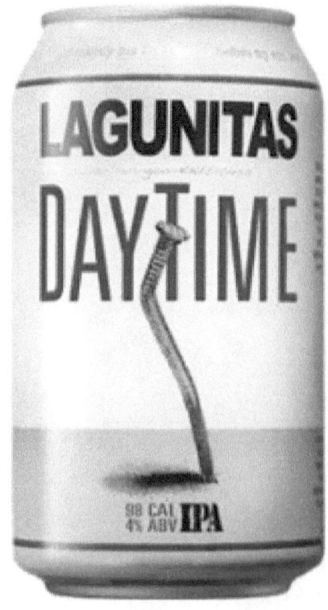

SESSION BEER

Now that we've established that wine can successfully coexist with baseball, let's talk a little about beer. Specifically, a session beer. What is that, you ask? It's as simple as it sounds: A session beer is light and easy-going.

It won't sit in your stomach like a shot-put. That makes this style ideal for mowing, movies, or any other occasion where just one won't do.

If you like IPAs, but you also enjoy pounding beers, then the **Daytime from Lagunitas** might be your beer soulmate. It has more body and hop than its pilsner cousins, meaning your taste buds have more to do while you're enjoying it. At 4% alcohol by volume (that's ABV in the biz) and 98 calories, this is a great no-fuss beer. You'll find hints of mango and grapefruit, not to mention a malty finish. If the goal is find something that goes down smooth, but isn't just beer-flavored water, the Daytime is the way to go.

8.

Monty Python and the Holy Grail (1975) -- Gewürztraminer

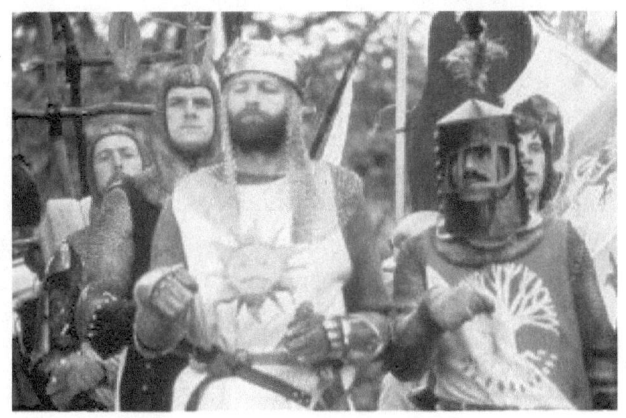

Monty Python and the Holy Grail stands as the most enduring artifact of the Pythons' comedic anarchy. Unlike their *Flying Circus* sketches, which were scatterbrained masterpieces that could mock anybody anywhere, *Holy Grail*drapes all of its hilarity over the same narrative clothesline. Beneath its shoestring budget lurks the highest of ambitions: Blood-soaked battles, lengthy animated sequences, elaborate musical numbers, and moments of flat-out gibberish. Few comedies have ever worked this hard in the name of drawing laughter.

The movie takes us to the grimy, soot-stained Dark Ages. King Arthur (Graham Chapman) and his loyal squire Patsy (Terry Gilliam) clippity-clop across the English countryside, hoping to recruit brave knights to join him at Camelot. Along this journey, Arthur meets Sir Lancelot (John Cleese), Sir Robin (Eric Idle), Sir Bedevere (Terry Jones), and Sir Galahad (Michael Palin). These men echo their historical counterparts, with the exception that they're, you know, morons. The image of God (actually W.G. Grace, a famous cricket player) appears in the sky, and commands Arthur and his lords to seek the Holy Grail.

Thus begins a bizarre odyssey, wherein the Pythons stitch together a series of comedic tangents that have become the stuff of cinematic lore: Arthur runs afoul of the Knights Who Say "Ni!", Galahad gets snared by a castle of randy sorority girls, and Lancelot finds himself rescuing a hostage-prince. Oh yeah, *and* there's the Black Knight. And Tim the Enchanter. And a Killer Bunny. Even at 92 minutes, this movie feels overstuffed with gags.

As with all the best Python humor, *Holy Grail* hides its audacity in plain sight. In lieu of actual horses, the actors bonk coconuts against each other, mocking both old-school foley and their own lack of budget. Most movies would get a few scenes worth of mileage of out this schtick before quietly retiring it. Not the Python boys. They beat the joke down for the entire length of the film, until you can't help but laugh at the sheer ballsiness of it. The troop also takes a page from *Blazing Saddles* by having the movie go meta. Arthur and his men ultimately realize they're in a film production, and a ramshackle one at that.

Per usual, each Python plays a host of varied characters. One of the most underrated things about this troop is their effortless chemistry. Watch the witch sequence to see how each actor reads and plays off the others. Everybody is outstanding, but this movie belongs to Chapman. His King Arthur is a noble buffoon–a pitiful man on an epic quest. Chapman anchors the film by playing straight man to the wackiness around him. Without his skill, the whole thing would founder.

While some movies hold up to multiple viewings, this is actually essential to *Monty Python and the Holy Grail*. So many jokes get fired in such rapid succession, it takes several trips on the ride to appreciate them all. Indeed, contemporary critics were bewildered by it, but the movie has grown in stature sense then. For everything that Monty Python has done, *Holy Grail* has become their definitive work. For me, it's the cinematic equivalent of comfort food. I can watch it over and over again, and its unabashed wackiness never seems to get old.

91 min. PG.

GEWÜRZTRAMINER

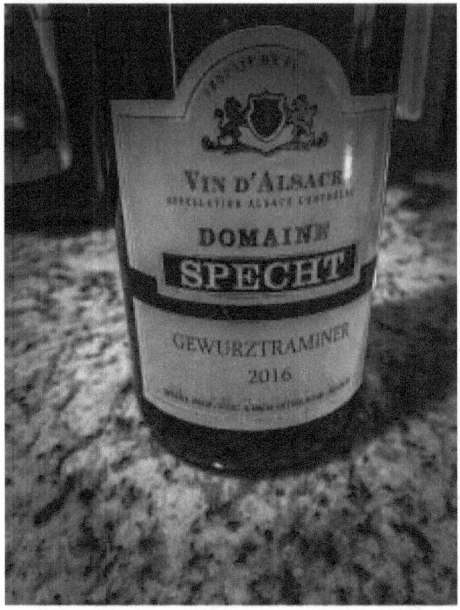

The first thing people always wanna know when they see this varietal is how to pronounce it. So, we'll get that out of the way: Guh-vertz-truh-meener. Give it a couple go-arounds and you'll have it.

Even though it has a long-ass name, the appeal of Gewürztraminer is pretty simple. It combines refreshing fruit flavors with a bit of a spicy kick. That makes this grape perfect for meals that might be otherwise difficult to pair: Spicy Asian and Mexican dishes go really well with Gewürz.

You're probably wondering what this grape has to do with *Monty Python and the Holy Grail*. Bear with me here: A classic argument in the film centers on how King Arthur and his brave knights acquire coconuts to knock together while they seek the Cup of Christ. Coconuts come from warmer climates, faraway from the damp chill of Great Britain. Could an African swallow have brought it from across the world? What about two swallows carrying it on a line? How fast would these little birds have to flap their wings to stay in the air? These are the questions that have plagued mankind for years.

Like those well-traveled coconuts, **Domaine Specht's Gewürztraminer** has a ton of tropical flavor, even though it can be found plunk in the Alsatian region of France. (That's a temperate zone, by the way.) The first thing you'll notice is an orchard's worth of orange flavor, followed closely by a pinch of zesty pepper. More fruits join the profile, including mangoes, pears, and peaches. The finish has a nice acidity, balanced with a smooth, creamy texture. Gewürz is a rarity in the wine world: It's approachable, but also complex and rewarding.

9.

The Remains of the Day (1993) -- Chablis

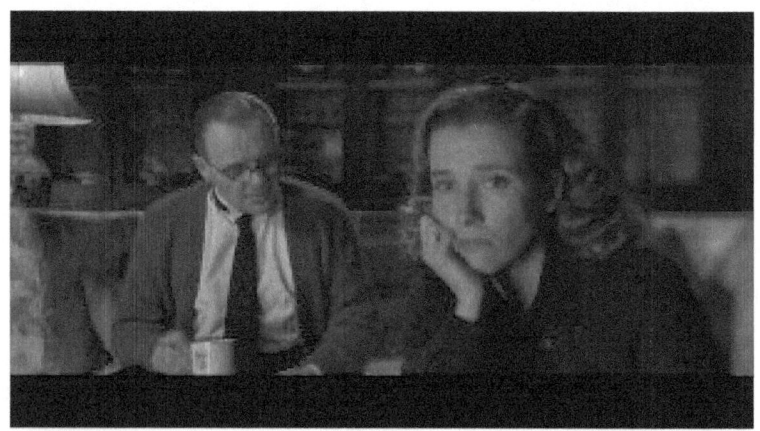

Columbia Pictures

An unwavering sense of duty cinches tight around the soul of James Stevens, the central character in *The Remains of the Day*. This singular focus makes Stevens an impeccable butler, but it also forms a tourniquet, choking off the pathways to love and happiness. Stevens takes great pride in his work until he finds, with great sadness, that the work is he has. Anthony Hopkins boasts a filmography filled with brilliance, but his performance as this tightly wound manservant stands tall. In the hands of Hopkins, Stevens is one of the most complex and tragic characters in all of cinema: He declares his occupational goal to make any room feel emptier by being in it, but this dedication renders the rest of his life empty as well.

The film moves between two timelines: In 1958, Darlington Hall, the manor where Stevens works, is being settled by Mr. Lewis (Christopher Reeve), a dashing American millionaire. Lewis dispatches Stevens to the English countryside to find a suitable housekeeper. Stevens reaches out to Sally Kenton (Emma Thompson), a charming, brilliant woman who filled the position many years ago. We then flashback to tumultuous, pre-WWII days, when the bustling house was headed by Lord Darlington (James Fox), a suave, genteel, and fatally misguided nobleman.

In their earliest days, Mr. Stevens and Miss Kenton don't get along much: She's too outspoken, too quick to smile, while he comes across as an icy, obsessive-compulsive prick. They clash when Stevens hires his senile, doddering father (Peter Vaughan) to work in the dining room, a duty for which Miss Kenton feels him unfit.

This rift paradoxically brings them closer: He is drawn to her warmth and compassion, and she believes his emotional stonemasonry hides something vulnerable and deeply human. As the years pass, Miss Kenton tries to shatter the bricks faster than Mr. Stevens can lay them. Their simmering love and loyalty get tested when it becomes apparent that Lord Darlington is a Nazi sympathizer.

Like its main character, *The Remains of the Day* moves with a methodical, meticulous pace. The relentless, chromatic scales in Richard Robbins' score give the film the steady march of a clock's second hand. Director James Ivory fills each scene with remarkable beauty and texture: Even when Stevens and Kenton stand in a downpour, it feels like a work of art. Ruth Prawer Jhabvala's script brims with intelligence, even if most of the characters use their overpowered vernacular to hide what they're really thinking.

That might be what makes this Merchant-Ivory production one of the greatest films ever made: So much of this story lies within feelings that can never be expressed or words that die on the tip of a tongue. Within the silence of this movie, you will find a gulf between what could be and what will never be. Mr. Stevens is a man who hides his pain and regret in plain sight. He aches, and we ache for him. *The Remains of the Day* is a film that will reward your patience with a frustrating, fascinating character study that seems to get better with every viewing.

134 min. PG.

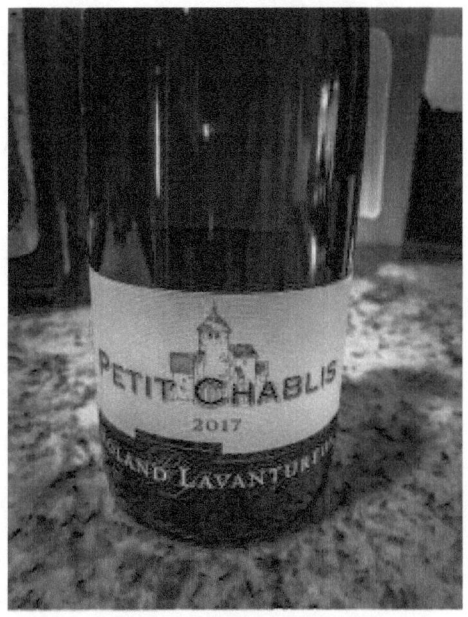

CHABLIS

Chablis is a white wine from the Burgundy region of north-central France. It is *always* 100% Chardonnay. Some of the most elegant, finely-crafted wines in all the world hail from this area. This makes it a perfect pair for the highfalutin intrigue in *The Remains of the Day*.

In the movie, snobs from around the world converge on Lord Darlington's estate to discuss geopolitical affairs. None of them would dare turn their nose up at a premium Chablis. When you pour and swirl a wine like this, feel confident that you're ready to mingle in the highest circles.

The Petit Chablis from **Domaine Roland Lavantureux** has all the classic traits of a French Chardonnay: It's crisp, clean, and has a refreshing acidity. You'll taste apples and pears on every sip, along with the limestone chalkiness that has become a trademark for whites from this part of the world. (This area was once a sea bed, and these fossilized minerals alter the texture and taste of the wine–in a very good way.) Also of note, this wine was aged in stainless steel barrels, further distinguishing it from the oaky butter-bombs you might find from California. If you're looking for a meal to match it with, Chablis is one of the few whites that will go with both surf *and* turf.

(Two quick notes: This wine is designated as a *Petit* Chablis, which means it's meant to enjoy now, rather than giving it a few years of age. Also, this one *might* exceed my $30 per-bottle budget by a smidge. If you love a good Chardonnay, this would be a great splurge wine. Pair it with a meeting of The Finer Things Club, or a high-end movie like *The Remains of the Day*.)

10.

Mad Max: Fury Road (2015) -- Pinot Noir

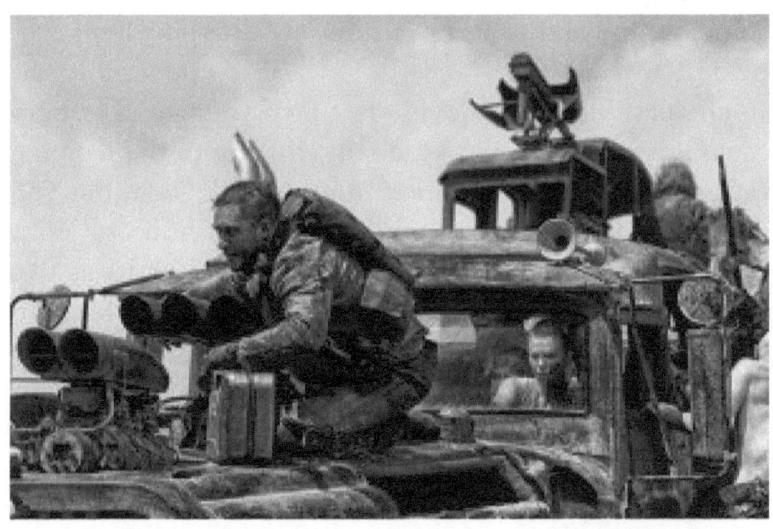

Photo by Jasin Boland – © 2012 Warner Bros.
Entertainment Inc
Mad Max: Fury Road creates a world of magnificent
desolation, where humanity skitters from one desperate

day to the next. The sun soaks the desert floor and whips molten winds across an ocean of simmering sand. The post-apocalyptic wasteland of this film serves as a character unto itself, forcefully prodding the characters to make frantic decisions in impossible situations. Critics tend to describe movies with histrionic hyperbole–a *non-stop thrill ride*, or *an all-out adrenaline rush*—but Mad Max: Fury Road delivers exactly that: The action isn't so much fast-paced as it is a dead, sweaty sprint, one that only occasionally allows the movie to gasp for air. This is the rare sequel–or soft reboot, whatever–that pays homage to its predecessors without strip-mining their legacy, and actually *builds on* what they accomplished by refining the qualities that made them great in the first place. *Fury Road* is a technical triumph of action and atmosphere that stands as one of the most exciting, jaw-dropping films ever made.

The first *Mad Max* movie–starring a young and hungry Mel Gibson–found mankind still clinging to the flapping tatters of civilization: Sure, things weren't great, but you could still see trees, grass, highways, and houses. With each successive film, the world looked less and less like what we now know and more like a superheated Martian landscape. By *Fury Road*, humanity is segregated into grubby little fiefdoms, each headed by its own monstrous warlord and each peddling its own basic neccessity–Gas Town, The Bullet Farm, etc. In the opening scenes, Max Rockatansky (Tom Hardy, who growls in a deep baritone) is captured by a particularly nasty despot named Immortan Joe (Hugh Keays-Byrne, who played the young biker villain in the first *Mad Max*). Joe is a burly, wheezing old man, his pasty body pocked with festering boils. Joe sends Furiosa (Charlize Theron, all bad-ass), one of his top lieutenants, on an errand to fetch supplies from the neighboring strongholds. What Joe doesn't know is that Furiosa has smuggled away his harem of young "breeder"-wives and is making a mad dash into the abyss. Max finds his way into Furiosa's convoy and the two form a tempestuous alliance to wriggle away from Immortan Joe's lecherous grasp.

If that sounds plot-heavy, it's not. Director George Miller—at the helm for every eccentric installment in the series—serves up a lean-meat Spaghetti Western masquerading as post-punk nihilism. Dialogue is so non-essential that Hardy's Max spends the first chunk of the movie muffled by a kinky metal mask. His Man with No Name takes a clear back seat to Furiosa, whose depth and humanity make her the movie's anchor. If Miller's opus has a clear flaw, it's that he never finds time to throw his protagonist on the stove to cook. Max spends the movie raw and waiting for a little seasoning that never comes. Like the movie, he's all visceral, all in the moment. Just a short scene or two of exposition—maybe with a smidge of actual dialogue—would've given a strong presence like Hardy a little more to do.

But that's a mild quibble. Most action movies are like dishwater—soggy and weighted with tired and tepid writing and direction. By comparison, *Fury Road* is fine and filtered Perrier, vibrant and relentlessly invigorating. Some may find it too adrenaline-soaked, too minimal, too *weird*, but there's no denying this movie is *alive*. The cinematography and editing (John Seale and Margaret Sixel, respectively) are as striking as any movie in recent memory. And *Fury Road*'s a rarity: Most sequels, remakes, and reboots are hollow cash-grabs, but Miller utilized his massive budget and a reservoir of patience to make the story he always wanted—a gorgeous, visually poetic action movie, set during a global Chernobyl.

120 min. R.

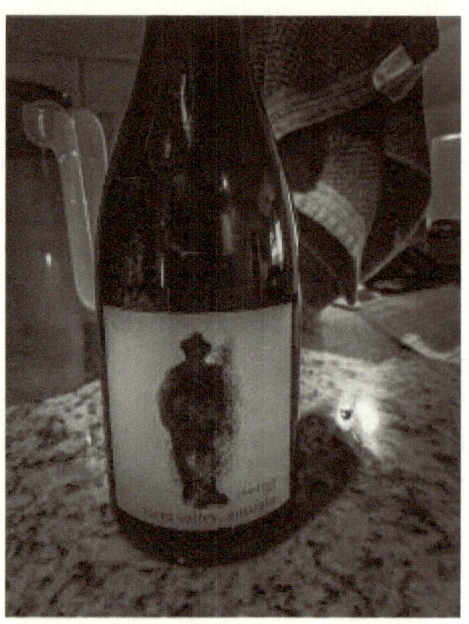

PINOT NOIR

Mad Max: Fury Road was mostly filmed in desolate stretches of Namibia, but there is no doubt this an Australian film. George Miller, the eccentric physician-turned-filmmaker who helmed all the films, infuses them all with an edgy, sneering sarcasm that represents the zeitgeist of early 80s Australian cinema. The world of Mad Max is wide open and filled with fascinating people. It's distinctly Down Under.

With that in mind, we'll pair this movie with a Pinot Noir from Australia. One way or another, every *Mad Max* movie involves innocents caught in a desperate crossfire. Ultimately, Max has to summon the last shred of his humanity and help people who can't help themselves.

That makes it appropriate for us to try this **Pinot from Innocent Bystander.** It has a lot of what people love about the grape: Bright cherry flavors are everywhere, along with hints of earthy, smoky notes. This has some body and complexity, but it's still an approachable, easy-drinking red. People struggle matching wines with holiday food–think turkey, dressing, cranberry, etc.–but Pinot Noir is always a no-brainer. It's also shies away from the tannins and dryness of heavier reds, making this a good entry wine for people looking to ease their way in.

I hope you've enjoyed this book! Please give me thoughts and feedback:

toddwofford@gmail.com